POETRY

November 2016

FOUNDED IN 1912 BY HARRIET MONROE

VOLUME CCIX · NUMBER 2

CONTENTS

November 2016

POEMS

RUTH LILLY AND DOROTHY SARGENT ROSENBERG POETRY FELLOWS

COMMENT

Editor	DON SHARE
Art Director	FRED SASAKI
Managing Editor	SARAH DODSON
Assistant Editor	LINDSAY GARBUTT
Editorial Assistant	HOLLY AMOS
Consulting Editor	CHRISTINA PUGH
Design	ALEXANDER KNOWLTON

COVER ART BY JESSIE MOTT
"Pegasus," 2016

POETRYMAGAZINE.ORG

A PUBLICATION OF THE
POETRY FOUNDATION
PRINTED BY CADMUS PROFESSIONAL COMMUNICATIONS, US

Poetry · November 2016 · Volume 209 · Number 2

Poetry (ISSN: 0032-2032) is published monthly, except bimonthly July/August, by the Poetry Foundation. Address editorial correspondence to 61 W. Superior St., Chicago, IL 60654. Individual subscription rates: $35.00 per year domestic; $47.00 per year foreign. Library/institutional subscription rates: $38.00 per year domestic; $50.00 per year foreign. Single copies $3.75, plus $1.75 postage, for current issue; $4.25, plus $1.75 postage, for back issues. Address new subscriptions, renewals, and related correspondence to Poetry, PO Box 421141, Palm Coast, FL 32142-1141 or call 800.327.6976. Periodicals postage paid at Chicago, IL, and additional mailing offices. POSTMASTER: Send address changes to Poetry, PO Box 421141, Palm Coast, FL 32142-1141. All rights reserved. Copyright © 2016 by the Poetry Foundation. Double issues cover two months but bear only one number. Volumes that include double issues comprise numbers 1 through 5. Please visit poetryfoundation.org/poetrymagazine/ submissions for submission guidelines and to access the magazine's online submission system. Available in braille from the National Library Service for the Blind and Physically Handicapped and from the Library of Congress. To request the braille edition, call 800-424-8567. Available on microfilm and microfiche through National Archive Publishing Company, Ann Arbor, MI. Digital archive available at JSTOR.org. Distributed to bookstores by Ingram Periodicals, Media Solutions, Ubiquity Distributors, Small Changes, and Central Books in the UK.

POEMS

BRENDAN GALVIN

An Egg Island Equinox

There is no radical shift of light
or redwings calling areas of marsh
their territories yet, nor plovers
probing for copepods. Only a yellow
front-end loader laying out a new berm
on the beach, from tubes too heavy
to be called hoses, its audience one man
and his protesting dog. No frosted
wedding cake on tour, no Cap'n
Beauregard hailing us from
the Texas deck, no Texas deck,
just an unshaven crew launching zodiacs
from the county dredge, its twin stacks
staining itself and the air with smoke,
as battered an emblem of hope as any other.
So spring comes to Egg Island, squealing
and unwilling. Sulfur and diesel,
flywheel, gear and grind until one morning
the equinox dawns and silences
the whole shebang.

An Example

Where can the dead hope
to stash some part
of themselves, if not in the living?

And so when I had a daughter,
I gave her your name.

She does not use it.

She goes by a silly, other
thing she was called once in fun,
and then often enough

that it stuck. But oh her hideous pill-
eyed toys — to them each, she has given
her given name,

and so it is you

I hear her again and again calling to.
It is your name she shrieks

to the bale-head farmer, the woven
goat, the cop made of buttons and rags.

Your name, to the squat gray

dog on wheels, tipping on its side
as she drags it by a red string.

That dog, always prone
and pulled along, as though constantly
being killed and paraded

through town to make an example.

What did it do—

Whatever it did, don't do it.

LAWRENCE JOSEPH

On Peripheries of the Imperium

I

Eye of the hurricane the Battery, the Hudson
breached, millions of gallons of it
north on West Street filling Brooklyn–Battery
Tunnel, overflowing into the World Trade Center site,
East River, six-to-eight-foot wall of water on South,
Front, Water, John, Fulton, Pearl,
Brooklyn Bridge's woven cables lifted delicately
in hurricane sky.

II

Perhaps I make too much of it, that time,
Eldon Axle, brake plates dipped
in some sort of liquid to protect them from
dust, dirt, metal chips the grinding caused —
that time, night shift, press-machine shop
on Outer Drive, rolls of stainless steel put in,
fixed up, because the work you do is around fire
your cuticles burn if the mask's not on right.

III

When the mind is clear, to hear the sound
of a voice, of voices, shifts in the attitude
of syllables pronounced. When the mind
is clear, to see a Sunday, in August, Shrine
of Our Lady of Consolation, Carey, Ohio,
at a holy water font, a mother washes
her six-year-old's fingers crushed in an accident
so that they'll heal.

IV

So what percentage of Weasel Boy's DNA
do you think is pure weasel? Tooth-twisted,
Yeats's weasels, in "Nineteen Hundred
and Nineteen," fighting in a hole.

V

Conflated, the finance vectors, opaque
cyber-surveillance, supranational cartels,
in the corporate state's political-economic singularity
the greatest number of children
in United States history are, now, incarcerated,
having been sentenced by law.

VI

A comic dimension to it, on this F train
to One Hundred Sixty-Ninth Street
in Queens? He doesn't want to disturb you,
but, see, he was stabbed in the face
with an ice pick, he lost his left eye —
lid pried open with thumb and forefinger —
here, look, he'll show you —
a white-and-pink-colored iris.

On Utopia Parkway

Between Grand Central Parkway and Little Bay,
from One Hundred Sixty-Ninth and Hillside

to Union Turnpike, to work — countless days the streets
I take to work. The front yard of roses —

did I write their names down correctly? —
Zephirine, Charis, Proud Land, Drouhin, Blale.

Q31 bus, among the words I hear are
Jamie, Jamie does not like to be humiliated,

Jamie is not about to forget it, either. Not
physically well, a poor man, arrested

on suspicion of selling cigarettes loose,
on the street, held, choked, left unconscious,

still handcuffed, no cardiopulmonary resuscitation
administered, pronounced dead, the cause of death,

according to the autopsy report, a homicide —
rectally infused puree of hummus, nuts, and raisins,

by employees of the Agency's contractor,
isn't torture, Director of Central Intelligence

explains, but, merely, legally justified means
of enhanced interrogation. 3708 Utopia Parkway

was Joseph Cornell's small wood-frame house.
He might have worked on the *Medici Slot Machine*

on his kitchen table, a Renaissance Box, a theater
he called it, the Medici and Mussolini's Fascist state

set in a metaphorical relation, its inner lines
the lines of the floor plan of the Pitti Palace,

the inclusion of an actual compass rose the expression
of an ascent from the temporal to the spiritual.

In what place, the Federal Reserve's
monetary spigots and banks' access

to cash pieced together with indexed futures, to reduce
the market's decline — in what places, violations

of which forms of which eternal laws?
Is it error, the idea that no place, too, is a place?

On the corner of Utopia Parkway and Union Turnpike,
in red-blue twilight abstracted into an energy

blowing it apart, in spaces of language transformed
and coded, to be decoded and recoded in the future.

STEPHEN BURT

Kites

Complete in ourselves,
we look like scraps of paper anyway:
        left alone, we could tell

our mothers and one another our owners'
        flimsiest secrets and play together all day

            until we became intertwined, which is why
you try
            to keep us permanently apart.

One of us is a gossamer pirate ship,
        a frigate whose rigging the industrial

            sunset highlights, sail by oblong sail.
Another resembles a Greek letter — *gamma*,
        or *lambda*; others still

a ligature, a propeller, a fat lip.
        Our will is not exactly the wind's will.
Underlined by sand,

            whose modes of coagulation and cohabitation
none of the human pedestrians understand,

we take off on our almost arbitrarily
        lengthy singletons of string

            towards the unattainable, scarily
lofty realm of hawk and albatross
        and stay, backlit by cirrocumulus.

            It seems to be up to you
to keep us
            up in the air, and to make sure our paths never cross.

ANNA MARIA HONG

English Mole

To push and push with raw pink claws like
hands of shin. To tunnel my love through wet
earth, wet stars — no one needs the underneath
like me. I give you permission to
grip me. To patrol the worm-drench of
my thinking. To bite a worm's head and cure
the rest as cache. Your flesh, my flesh, your dead
as dead, buried like a feeling. To push through
that wet, a scrum of worms whittling
my skin like a premonition. To have pushed
mountains into hills, ragged sooth from the
slid wall of healing. "Nothing,"
said the suicide, "is as sad as recovery."
To work myself forward like a noun or an entry.

BENJAMIN GOLDBERG

Dog Head

Our mascot was the bulldog. Bulldogs chased me across playgrounds
until I dreamed them. In class, I finished mazes with a green crayon.
Hedges grew skyward from pages, and I ran. My dad once called
this kind of thing my day-head. When my day-head happened,
they called him at his office. I learned the name *Daedalus* from an
    article
I read for science class. It meant a plane with leg-powered wings —
carbon tubing, plastic skin. A man with a long name flew a longer way
across the sea from Crete. At recess, I reread the same book
of illustrated myths and cryptids. I dreamed of bulldogs with bulls'
    heads.
My day-head was a zoo where gods slept. *Daedalus* sounded like *dad*,
so I loved him. Class was an enclosure made of cinder block
and twelve weeks without winter. Behind the glass, my day-head
    paced.
Daedalus was a zookeeper. I dreamed of a god with a bull's body
and a hood sewn from my face. The article said I weighed the same
as the *Daedalus*. I traced flight plans and crash sites on my desk.
My teacher asked us to draw self-portraits. The trees were hydras.
On the paper, I drew an outline of my face. I cut my eyes out
with scissors. They called me to the office, and Daedalus was waiting.
I found a bulldog in a magazine and drew a maze inside each iris.
We played tug-of-war in gym. My day-head was a knotted rope
dangling from steel rafters. I pushed my thumb into the sun. I fell
    once.
I cut the bulldog from the page, then ripped his head in two.
I glued one half over the left side of my face. I left the right side
    blank.
The article said the *Daedalus* crashed twenty-one feet from the black
    sand
of a beach on Santorini. My day-head was a Kevlar fuselage
belly-down in the sea. They called home. I ran home.
On the right side of my face, I drew a sunny day. I signed my name.

JACK UNDERWOOD

Instead of Bad News about a Person I Love

I got a letter through the post decreeing my sainthood.
Beatified, I sat down, because this was big news for me.
Bless the television, bless this chair of four wooden legs.
I felt like calling my parents, but thought, in a saintly way,
to do so would be immodest, so instead I opened the curtains.
Rain was washing everything that seemed in need of washing.
A bird landed on a bush and shook water from its wings
and I closed my eyes briefly, acknowledging its small,
hardworking soul, like a microchip destined for heaven.
The cat came in, little devil, and I forgave her, touching
under her chin, sweet child. We watched the news together
and reflected that this was how the world churns
its butter of beginnings and endings in front of the sun.
What good, I wondered laterally, might befall an ancient
tree today? Perhaps merely nothing much. Perhaps a tree
will carry on just as it was. What minerals will develop
unseen in the earth, deep beneath a human tragedy?
Some minerals. Some salty, bright minerals in the dark.
I spent that morning cutting white paper into triangles.
I spent that afternoon staring at my bits, enamored.
I spent that evening clapping loudly in the garden,
and come bedtime I was ready to write my long email
to the President of the United States of America.

I'm on the boating lake with Sean

I'm gently rowing and the birds look sewn
to the surface of the water as it undulates to the sound
of Sean talking beautifully about something
I don't really understand. But all I'm picturing
are brown paper bags with little grease spots near
the bottom seams that have recorded the way
sausage rolls have touched them, or the thin waists
of dogs as depicted in medieval hunting frescos, or
a cherub's fat little hand gesturing
to a vista where smiling families are meeting
to picnic with the animals that God
has also saved, or I'm thinking about
the mechanics of bagpipes, the legs and arms
and the fat belly and the long neck with its holes.
This has been the best day ever. Sean smiles.
He's wearing shorts, and so am I.
It's sunny! Mine are so short
they may as well be underpants, and I still
don't understand a word that he is saying.

Totem Pole

I put an animal on an animal
which I put onto the animal I had already stacked
on top of my first animal and stood back
to appraise my work only
it looked much too short despite the number
of animals I had gathered, and I felt tired and silly
and disappointed, slumping to my knees, rocking
back onto my bum, then lying down to stare
into the hoary sky until my eyeballs softened
and I was forced by the consistent light
to close them and listen to the animals taking
a surprisingly long time to disorganize themselves.

The Man with the Blue Guitar

His blue guitar is lacquered so brightly when he leans
a certain way into his song I can see my head in my hands
reflected. And when he leans back into the emotion
of another chorus his guitar returns to blue: the blue
of unboiled lobsters fading to a general Biro-lid blue
and with a patina of fine tiger stripes the color of sky
midway towards a springtime horizon. I've had a long
time to consider this.

The man with the blue guitar has a little tin for his plectrums,
with a cartoon pelican on its lid, standing on top of the words
"Pelican Throat Lozenges." Between songs he tells me
that he found it in the abandoned house from the song.
Which song? My next song. It's called "The Abandoned House."

The man with the blue guitar reads his lyrics from a special
leather book where he has written all his lyrics.
Sometimes he forgets the words and searches the page
as he plays, his face scrunching as he sings new noises
in their place. I prefer the noises. *This song is called
Halloween Moon this song is called Lovesick Bougainvillea
this song is called Bourbon Canal this song is called
St. Michael's Boots My Cousin's Old Coat The Wrestler's
Arm The Old Arm Wrestler Dead Man's Stetson
Panama Morning The Skulls of the Cathedral Lawn
Shadow in the Gully in the Foothills of My Youth
My Heart Is a Love Letter the Folds Are Worn Through.*

If I seem too pleased each time he finishes he takes it
as an invitation to play another song. If I do not seem
pleased enough each time he finishes his determination
only reaches further through his face and so he plays
Saratoga Skyline or *Sad Preacher's Walk* or *The Lonely
Way to Gypsy Street* or *The Story of Your Life* or

The Story of the Man with the Blue Guitar
which is the story behind this, my next song.

MICHELLE MITCHELL-FOUST

Camera Eulogia

Herodotus says the king made a bowl to leave behind
the memory of a number. We don't know the number.
We don't know if it was divisible by two or three.
I want, at the moment, the number to indicate
a ratio, part of a proportion, because the measurement
of the earth depends on this, the balance among things,
the snow at the bottom of the hill, the gold garage light
caged in a tree, my love for my friend and the distance
between us, which I can't bear.

I made a pinhole camera to demonstrate proportion,
and everything bright hovers on its milky eye,
and here is the catalogue of what hovers there
smaller than itself: the blue horizon and the dash
at the stoplight, a shell night-light, the gazing ball
of the sun going down against the white back fence,
which made it look like night in the woods lit
from underneath on the wax. I held these things
yesterday, along with two pearls that are spheres
hanging from my living room ceiling.

My friend is smaller now, and if I held my camera up
to her, she would give off enough light to hover
pocket-sized in my hand, and grand in the world.

VI KHI NAO

Tarragon, Are You a Wild Boar?

Tarrargon, are you a wild boar?
My friend, lemon zest, has not been that
Thyme, Cognac, *falooda* glass noodle
These things prowl the night without cape
Gooseberries or bacalao

Tarragon, are you a wild boar?
Each time I eat you, I stop breathing
Little owl, where is your happiness?
Wake up + make people believe
In you, gastrique + steaklette
Is that chive embarrassed?
To be with the savoy cabbage?

Tarragon, are you a wild boar?
I was born female, hyper-focused
Let me trim your skirt, halibut
It's dragging salt against my oregano
Buttered by butter in no butter

Tarragon, are you a wild boar?
It's too bad the caper isn't wearing
A cape when the Peruvian potatoes
Are sitting on a bed of coals while
Floating down a river coconut
On the verge of falling off
A truffle, which is a
Shadow floating inside of a shadow

Fish Carcass

fish carcass
say hello to pork rind
+ arborio rice
while castaway caraway puree returns
home to deconstruct wilted carrot
from its butter + herb remnants

fish carcass
say goodbye to a knife fight
between under-marinated onion slice
+ wasted redbor kale
amidst a gun battle between
grilled salmon + paprika

fish carcass
say goodnight to electrolytes + magnesium
as a chemical imbalance takes
place inside the borderline cod meat

fish carcass
say good morning to anti-griddle + orange liqueur
whose pre-conditional love for salt + bitterness
reminiscent of caviar + pancetta vinaigrette
has put quail eggs
under the cloche

fish carcass
say midday to emu eggs while
the sun twirls
inside a decadent basket of
fish sauce without making
the plastic mattress, walk-in
refrigerator, + bacon sabayon
feel left out

fish carcass
say cloud nine
say egginess
say shell-shocked
say cornichon
say it angelo
say italian meringue
say calf liver
say republic of georgia
say lavash
say turnpike turnips
say succotash
say yuzu marmalade
say overcooked quail

say chef teah evans
say fish head
say into a barrel
say bacon fat
say baby corn
say flavor profile
say with victory
say the gods are with me
say no guts no glory
say did not materialize
say story on a plate

ADAM FITZGERALD

Low Impact Fat Burning Workout

How does one grow the cojones to celebrate a Fudgsicle?
I'll tell you, and won't begin by mentioning trellises forsooth.
The items on the register are mechanisms inscrutable, yes.
But they sway in the doubled-up air with a sense of lucidity,
A kind of gong affect that chiggers as it steamrolls forth,

Appraisals for unchintziest bling. Time for a sea change.
Your turn, and this means you
Come with me. Agreeable and mute, like the original
Doppelgänger, or as we in my neighborhood called it
The Doppler Radar.

On school mornings, a trust fund in my teeth,
High yacht vanilla swilled my parents' bed.
I would be multiple and exact.
From that vantage, a windpipe brought forth
On invisible horseback to the sick child's bed.

I'm sure you can't quite imagine it, ember
In the tabby lobby. But I could. I arrested it.
Gershwin and American Airlines and I could always
Tell the voice without the face, God's gift to me
For being lame in phlegmatic tissue. O parabola.

Look at the ashtrays! There they are. Swinging, roiling,
Ocean-choppy, a gauntlet of remote controls,
Paint supplies all stacked up with nowhere to go
In the corner of a grave illness — like pink paint.
This forecast of centenarians in Florida, and Burbank.

All my life I wanted a fractal tie and strawberry apron.
Now I'm a Church lady, no hint of arthritic condition.
My name isn't Sallie or Mae, it's Sallie Mae.
Millions of tiny pendants, Waterford crystal, bubbling
From local tree-fort where boys grope one another.

Will you come with me for Pilates at Fort Ticonderoga?
Denise Austin is here. Stretch in the sun.
Champagne woods, lakes chasms, dismounts.
Then you say: You have no idea what I lived through.
The Green Mountain Boys were like a second dad to me.

ROBIN RICHARDSON

The Most Expensive

Figured marry for money the stainlessness of it
thermostatic shower simulates but isn't rain
I simulate rain too. I do lines off a photo
of the lunar landing he says is make-believe
I don't know the difference most of the things
most of the time are as if our Brooklyn Bridge
selfies aren't faked to goad our favorite exes
as if my diet of carrots and cayenne is 'cause
nothing tastes as good as skinny makes money
makes the bed and stands beside us like a parent
with poor boundaries who just wants us
to be happy. Mommy's money takes her
to Key West where she sends pictures of a cat
on king-sized everything says *Hemingway
had money, honey!* Figured I'd money myself
into perpetuity as if anything weren't working
back to nothing. Figured marry but got thinking
now the money keeps itself to itself in Park Slope
in a Whole Foods growing greener.

DONALD REVELL

The Glens of Cithaeron

Till the gold fields of stiff wheat
Cry "We are ripe, reap us!"
— Ted Hughes

I begin to think Actaeon never changed.
The words that followed him, the poems
That leapt upon him and left him for dead
Were difficult exactly to the extent
They were rational. It makes perfect sense
For nakedness to give way to frenzy.
And the poems, let's be clear, were naked.

Time was, questions were put, clear as water.
The Goddess bathed, and time was the soft smile
Of water catching the sunlight on her.
And the sunlight, let's be clear, was sheer murder.
Into the same creature, no human word
Leaps twice. Given to frenzy, nakedness
Smiles upon the breaking of men and dogs.

How easy to lose all patience with chaste things!
Christ, I am hoping to hear from you
Before the hunters and suicides make off with me.
Christ, I am hoping to take your weapons
To a tarn freezing in the death of me.
I shall harry the moon there. I shall halloo.
Bayed in the cross-tree is a lion too.

In 1969 a red stag made
A cobweb of moonlight in his antlers.
For once in your life, pray without ceasing,
Pray the stag safely by the lion's tree.
Actaeon never changed. Predator
Is simply prey to nakedness and reason.
The poems have been out hunting all the time.

Then it is Friday. Frisk. You might as well.
Seeing as the rapeweed, you might as well.
The lion is no stranger. The belling
Stag is as familiar as the moon, but a strange
Suicide. Taken by legs, taken
By sinews, kissing the cobwebs of moonlight,
He prays the prayer I was not quick to say.

Berries and hoardings, ermine horseplay short
Of the new, short of poems no longer old
As I knew them, leaving the small schools
For the main campus rapeweed climbing, pale.
It is Friday. Stars won't cross. Actaeon
Never imagined the frail, sheer speed
Of meat. Christ, eat me. Nothing else makes sense.

On the far
Safe side of becoming,
Metaphor

Is all love,
The pure being of each
Nude above

Perfect sense.
I begin to hunt words.
The tension

The soft smile
Of the Goddess eases
A short while

Reappears
In a red stag's terror.
Metaphor

Leaps and eats.
It is not difficult.
Love is meat.

The dogs leap on Actaeon. He is human.
I begin to think of Time as anything
In the gift of humans or as sacrifice
To the long uplift of lions in the blood.
Now dogs tear deeply into the living flesh.
Each moment is a visible agony,
And still the godly human nature remains

Unharmed. I never imagined the sheer frail
Of fear so powerful. Legs and sinews turn
Into flowers. Between her breasts, the Goddess
Shelters one such, one blood violet alive.
The porch of heaven is littered with color.
As familiar as the moon, our humanness
Crosses into heaven as the new poem.

On the far side of becoming, a life's work
Begins another kind of work, but naked
Of change. There are animals, water and trees.
Nothing is recognizable in its old
Skin, yet everything shimmers. I am afraid,
Shrinking from the teeth of the cold water
And from the howling trees. I perish at this point

Down among dogs and upwards beside lion.
The pieces of me are carried fast away
By plot and rhyme. See Artemis bathing.
The moonlight on her body is the mother
Of God. It makes perfect sense. I am eaten
And fed changeless into her breast, blood
Violet alive. I remain your friend.

Subway Ride, Spring 2002

The train moved me, clothes kept me seated.

I watched the tunnel walls blur and my face appear, nicer on black plexiglass.

The people carried off like I almost was

in the old childhood dream, my mother's hand, the tornado in the parking lot.

Flooring soda and rain, a humble poser, a composed consumer.

Come back to me, I whispered to the purifying wind in a country I'd visited years earlier.

Come get me, I said to imaginary John Lennon in the passenger seat of my 1984 Volvo.

Nothing grows anywhere, I noted in the slick urine grime connecting two underground stations.

As for my wallet, it was light in my hand, fictitious, I didn't deserve it —

I held it up in the crowded terminal like a magician's pigeon.

Or I hid it between my knees on the jerking seat.

Nobody wanted to touch me, or

nobody who wanted to could reach me here,

shaken like a screaming child under wet stairs.

"Come Godard, come, here, Godard, here ..."

A cento

Is there no when where this dream will rest?
   Blue smoke, wings, a plague
of walls, the city motionless, mass
   of mind and angst rising
in the brilliance of a cloudless light
    [*le ciel, c'est mauve comme la lavande*].

Everything turns in the quiet leisure of disaster:
   a kind of innocence
now supernatural darkness floating,
   trees shaking, waterways
swollen under a livid sky, storm clouds
   forming in the blink of an eye.

The thought of you is performative: blonde
   hair, pale complexion, downcast
jewels for eyes. Your dreadful martyrdom
   runs its course, written in mud
and butter: the human instant, in which
   you sing yourself full-throated.

Honey, ginger, flared saffron, graywhite
   momentous rhythm of sea,
barbarous smell of wet earth, ransacking
   or ravaged flowers, the landfill
site, shit-hole, killing ground from which we sup
   as shaking, hiccuping drunks.

To forfeit wisdom, atone for sins undone:
        the allegorical
hand thrust into torture, noise, shadows
        of men. Between the lines,
against the clock, this does not make,
        does not make a difference to them.

This age [*our* age] demands an image of its
        accelerated grimace —
an old bitch gone in the teeth, the ultimate
        cunt — our botched
civilization, our grave in the sky: last jizz
        of consciousness.

I could have, now, blown my fucking brains out,
        but for a sweet shimmer of reason,
blood, lone bells in gritty belfries, the shallows
        of the sea, the surprise of days
which slide under sunlight, the soul
        gathered up, exhaled as rings of smoke.

Clay is the word and clay is the flesh. You
        drape your body against
my body, like a sheet of mirrored glass;
        you remain, *comme le dit*
Flaubert, melancholique devant son rêve accompli.
        — The word "red" is not.

Forever in lust, forever in heat of fire and flood.
     Mule-bray, pig-grunt, bawdy
cackle and the stomping of feet to the beat
     of some undone family portrait
— bad teeth, bad eyes, beer and paint cans —
     the name and date split in soft slate.

Money makes an inverse difference
     to distance, when I lift her back
to me now: nothing there but that pale
     curly head, working
a machine up and down, an ochre
     autumn merging into twilight.

I read much of the night. Guns click and spit
     and split up timber, until
the river's tent is broken: old kettles, old
     bottles, a broken can, old iron,
old bones, old rags, that raving slut
     who kept the till.

Dreams nourished with tears, the sweet kinks
     of fists, light rain falling as mist.
The hours after you are gone are a lead
     white morning of hard, new ice,
the snow drift of that which is left unspoken.
     Care and great sadness are both a burden.

No gods, but a black swastika and no sky
        but grinding water, gasping
wind, the wares of carthage, girls
        with peacock eyes. The churn
of stale words staining the heart again:
        bleached wood massed as bones.

Your body is white as anemone petals,
        your skin is stone smooth, we
[as cold as the dead they load
        like a pile of baskets, mound
of refuse, the sweepings of a street]
        are pressed close together, swaying.

Merely the despaired occasion of wordshed
        made keener by blessed rage.
Scrape away the prison coating, the itchy
        sea; drink from this glass
of pure, real, resplendent blood, its
        malediction, freshly soiled and snug.

It's a question of altitude, probably, walking
        along your eyelid again, towards
your tear duct. This dance of fire
        that touches our lips, scorches
our tongues and pulls out the thin
        beaten tin of my squally voice.

O technosociety, where memory is tolerated,
        barely, as real estate
on which to mount steeples of rust, lay
        fresh mowed grass, burn gasoline:
anything so long as there's a margin
        and little but commerce between us.

We never have pure space in front of us, rather:
        slight bondage, the world's halter,
this fashion for dressing or setting our hair
        ablaze until we're ash and ash
in the heat of a blank but infinitely scrolling
        screen, flared back to scratch.

We begin and end with a groan, the tongue's
        comfortable wetness, sureness
of soul and fluttering lips. Then:
        lords of unquiet, quiet sojourn,
each atom which belongs to you
        belongs to me.

All abandoned, the last rig broken, the staggering
        shadows of trees, fence posts, gutted
cars, faces blurred and Sienese grave.
        I wish that I could speak only
of it all, the voices of children singing.
        A chapel, in spite of it all.

After Ashbery, Auden, Baudelaire, Beckett, Berryman, Bunting, Carlos Williams, Carson, Carson, Celan, Creeley, Dickman, Dupin, Éluard, Eliot, Elliott, Fisher, Forché, Forest-Thompson, Frost, Ginsberg, Grünbein, Gunn, Harsent, Hill, Kavanagh, Levertov, Levine, Lowell, MacNeice, Mallarmé, Middleton, Muldoon, Phillipson, Plath, Pound, Prynne, Reading, Riley, Rilke, Rimbaud, Stein, Stevens, Verlaine, Waldron, Whitman, Williams, Wright, and Yeats.

ISABEL GALLEYMORE

The Ash

like a single branch of ash
honed to the handle of an axe
and made to take the hand
of a woodsman as he throws
his body weight to fell
all the ash has sown,
I turn your words although
the line you spoke was simple

Seahorse

Isn't it shocking how he speaks for her?
His thin voice wavering across the restaurant —
she'll have the cod artichoke bake.

A giggle of bubbles comes from behind them:
a fish tank curtained with seagrass
where a seahorse is tying itself
to one of those slim, tweedy forms

like a hand shaping itself inside another's
the way my hand tucks into his
like a difference pretending it's not.

DONNA MASINI

Mindscreen

See, it's a kind of crime scene,
as if the mind were a dime
novel, a scrim of need and semen,
all cinder and siren, a dim
prison where the miser dines
on rinds of desire, and the sinner,
sincere as denim, repeats Eden's
demise — that luckless toss of dice.
Yet here at the rim of this demesne
a mitigating mise-en-scène:
a close-up of her mother stirring rice,
a glass of sparkling cider, a mince
pie spliced in — not to rescind or mend:
what mind denies mercies mine in the end.

LESLIE McGRATH

Nowhere Near Hudson's Bay

Toggle me up
on one last vanity flight
half drunk on a screw-top *frizzante*.
It takes a hell of a lot more to get me here
than it did when I had beauty, boys
when bedding me was the easy way to know me.

Don't tuck me in
so tight. I'm not your grandma.
This rough blanket
its green red yellow indigo stripes
I traded for a perfectly warm beaver pelt.

Fly me once more
over my disloyal youth
and its hangdog slavering over men
whom age has de-sexed right along with me.
They broadcast impotent outrage
from aluminum tablets.
I collect speculums with Bakelite handles
arranging them by size
though it no longer matters.

A well-stocked pantry

My wife went into the pantry for peaches
but came out with a baby — I hadn't noticed
the house was pregnant, she said —
it was crying, so I cried back —
then she cried, the woman I barely know
after sixteen years — why just the other day,
she told me she'd always been afraid
#2 pencils might be made
of what they're named — but even crying
it was cute — pink and scrunchy-eyed —
like a newt balloon someone had blown up
until puffy and ready to pop —
it was as if the universe decided
it was time to act our age — that's
when we threw all our heroin out —
took the high-wire down and stopped
skeet shooting in the living room —
and as much as I miss yelling *Pull*
while stoned and standing on the edge
of the air, looking into the abyssal fall
I sorta desperately want, someone's
gotta change the diapers and burp the thing
when it fills with swamp-gas or whatever
that is — the miracle, you know, of birth
is that my wife and I gave up hang gliding
for making the nummy sound against the belly
of the beast who showed up and took over —
just as once, I shot the rapids, popped out,
squirmed against my mother and destroyed
every other future she might have lived
but one — long before I could speak,
I was cruel — for a few seconds,
I let my mother believe I was everything
she ever wanted — and even now, decades after
my few perfect seconds as a baby, if I called,

at the first unexpected brush of *Hey, ma*
against her ear, she'd still be hoodwinked
by the tidal pull of my voice
on the ghost of a womb they long ago
ripped out, that she was holding
a full moon in her arms

CONOR O'CALLAGHAN

Trailer Park Études

THE STARS

The nights midweek are secrets kept.
No soul on site, no signal/bars,
and zilch for company except
a zillion bright disarming stars.

I'll flit through ambers, quicker, higher.
I'll break each hamlet's STOP or YIELD.
I'll fix some noodles, start a fire
and climb up to the topmost field.

The stars at first are sparse, unclear.
They surface in that drag between
the darkened grass and stratosphere,
of powder blue and bottle green.

They blossom, thick and fast, in droves.
They pulse, in clusters, magnify.
The smoke that's my potbelly stove's
frays outwards through each needle eye.

I'll head below. I'll char till dawn
some apple logs down to their core.
By pewter light when stars have gone,
I'll do a bit, a little more.

THE RAIN

You live inside its sound effects
whole weeks on end: its pin machine,
its cardboard drum, its soft-boiled eggs,
its silent running submarine.

It's like the god of liquid rub-
ber stirred at dawn to slip downstairs
and sip a cigarette, to drub
his fingertips on solid layers

you poured across last summer's drought.
You love it, learn to, as it slows,
and even as you come to doubt
its dribs and drabs and pigeon toes.

Forget the welcome rain outstayed.
For days the leaves are parchment sheet
and wind hangs chimeless in the shade.
Still rain remains the point of heat.

The rain is near. Like everything,
it's best those seconds just before:
the broadleaf's backwards canvas sling,
the fly strip flapping through the door.

THE WIND

The wind's this ancient bloke below
who chunters "we," who wheezes "us,"
though no one else will come or go.
You want to ask the wind "Who's *us*?"

but hold your tongue till, in your head,
the wind and him have somehow mixed,
the type of wind that loves a shed
and banging on of things not fixed:

a belt-and-braces year-round wind,
a kiln-dried cobwebbed hardwood wind,
a greenhouse wind, a treebound wind,
an end-of-season car-boot wind,

a padlocked shower unit wind,
an upturned wheelie dumpster wind,
a channel not quite tuned-in wind,
a hollow flight-path thunder wind,

a dog-eared wind, a knocked-sign wind,
a spouseless phantom ocean-blown
autumnal graveyard Scots pine wind
who speaks in plurals, moves alone.

THE GRASS

One night last June, in cups, in love
with pickled gin from bubbly flutes,
our clothes in coils about the stove,
we climbed the dark in birthday suits.

It's true! The grass was mown that day.
Like hippies chained in meadow flowers,
we tripped above the cut and lay
in blades of petrol suede for hours.

We listened to the lowing black.
We giggled, kissed. We possumed dead.
We woke as flesh and straggled back
like beasts for parlor, dressed, then read.

We trafficked grass in bedspreads, shoes,
and never spoke of that again
through winter's interregnum blues,
of being spooked by skin, of when

the only care we had was grass,
the only stir for miles around
our freezing bones, our clinking glass,
our dying to be rumbled, found.

CLAUDINE TOUTOUNGI

Future Perfect

The Linguisticator meets you at Carrefour.
Un vrai galant, he buys you *rouge à lèvres*.
Teaches socially accepted forms of extrication.

If someone gropes you, say *Arrête tes bêtises*.
If someone wonders why your hair is mussed, say *C'est le mistral*.
If someone asks you to admire their ugly baby, say *Je me sauve*
    and leave.

The Linguisticator is a veritable language experience.
You programmed him in Oregon but he caught a virus.
Now his Frenchness is *cent fois* off the spectrum.

Sings Aznavour as you tour the *centre historique* and Piaf on the
    tram;
Padam, Padam, when it clangs.
The Linguisticator can stop a tram with one raised eyebrow,

one *soi-disant* eyebrow. A fatalist, he has abandoned caution
with certain potent liquors of the region. Ask him if he's OK,
    he'll say
Le silence éternel de ces vastes espaces m'effraie.

Ask him what irony means, he says
Tout pour le mieux dans ce meilleur des mondes possibles.
But if his ennui peaks, he suspends all conversation.

Broods for hours muttering *Putain,*
je suis rien qu'un two-bit trompe l'œil.
Malaise on a loop. It never fades.

New Born

The first thing I did against my will is see light.
Older, in my mother's belly with a good mind,
I sometimes dreamed different kinds of darkness.
I kicked, had sweet dreams and nightmares
something like death, unborn happiness,
blind hallucinations, memories I can't name
that still push me to act with unborn hands,
all before breathing.

What last thing will cross my mind
after last rights and wrongs?
They say the grand finale is like sleep,
I may feel love's nuts and bolts unscrewing—
it's best to be held tight. A pillow does not kiss.
May I never waver in peaceful unmindfulness.
I've seen passionate suffocation,
I've felt exquisite pain. Far better doggerel:
"Nurse, nurse, I'm getting worse!"
Undone, I'd like my last thoughts to rhyme:
> I did not lend
> you my love. The end.

A Poem Called Day

Day is carved in marble, a man reclining,
a naked giant suffering.
Preoccupied Day faces Night, who is a woman,
huge, naked, Herculean, both pillowed
on their uncarved rough marble bed.
They need light to be seen, neither
has anything to do with the sun or moon.
Art is not astronomy,
but the heavens are useful as gardening to poets,
not useful as love or loneliness.
If I write out of arrogance and ignorance
a poem called Day, my chisel and mallet, words
and pen, paper my marble, I must not confuse
sunlight and Day, petals with hours. I could rhyme,
perhaps by reason and chance describe the nature of Day.
I might discover Nature is surprisingly
sometimes moral, unexpected, a principle
over which the lovers Night and Day quarrel.

In my poem, faithful Night and faithful Day quarreled;
rhyme told me they quarreled because Day is gold,
Night hates the thought of celestial money,
rages at the starless differences between cost and price.
Michelangelo did not choose to make a sculpture
Prezzo, or put the finger of God on a coin.
Day and Night saw Danaë's legs spread apart
for Zeus to enter as a shower of gold.
They are not household gods or saints.
Better I write about things nearby,
a chair, a stool, the principle I'm sitting on.

Day is my dictionary. If my Day were animal, he might be
a baby elephant who eats leaves.
My good Day stays close to his mother,
who is murdered for her ivory tusks.

My Day is an endangered specie. I whisper
into elephant ears, *peace, my darling little Day*.
An owl hoots, *your Day has no given name!*
True, I refuse names useful to many others:
Sabbath, Sunday, Friday, Saturday.
My Day is not baptized, circumcised, or blessed.
I pick him up and hold Day in my arms.
I put my head in Day's open mouth.
I tongue Day, and Day tongues me.
Yes, although my Day loves Night,
he tongues me in and out of bed.
My Day knows Night carnally,
lets Night know me.
So I love Day today.
And I love Night tonight.

Idling

There's wondering, idle thoughts,
thinking over what was last said,
some poetry in my head
like traffic outside the window.
In my forgetful marrow, I consider
often lying words, like *everything* and *all*.
Nothing is another matter.
Nothing comes of everything and all.
Something comes of nothing.
I know the word *no* means no,
yes, yes, except when they mean each other.
There's *water*, which means water,
dishwater, that may mean worthless.
It's often better
to say *worthless* when you mean it.
I've come to *meaning*, that can mean
reason for or *reason to live*,
words I might say outright
without first saying *meaning*.
Then there is a mean man.
How did *mean* come to have two meanings?
Take a dictionary of homonyms
and tell me how words got to sound alike
with different meanings and spellings,
a Sea of Words
which is a Chinese dictionary.
Language has its ways,
its altitude and latitude ...
Stanley, baby, quit jerking on and off.
I'm simply talking to myself.
I am more familiar with the dark night
and bright day of the body
than the dark night of the soul.
Light has an exaggerated reputation.
Goethe's last words were, "*Mehr Licht!*"

Faust was dragged off to hell
when he was content.
Goethe preferred discontent, which needed light.
The seed is contained discontent.

SHANE McCRAE

Jim Limber the Adopted Mulatto Son of Jefferson Davis Was Another Child First

They put me in a dead boy's clothes dead Joseph

Except he wasn't dead at first they put

Me in his clothes dead Joseph's   after Joseph

Died and I used to call him Joe   they put

Me in Joe's clothes at first before he died

Joe wasn't five yet when I met him   I

Was seven   I was seven when he died

Still but a whole year bigger then but I

Wore his clothes still and the whole year I lived with

Momma Varina   and with daddy Jeff

I never lived so good as when I lived with

Them and especially it was daddy Jeff

Who kept me fed and wearing those nice clothes

Until they fit as tight as bandages

Inhospitable

Each time the babies came
I knew they would be gone
by morning.

Bright as bulbs
turned out of beds,
hard and full
of promise.

Bodies
on the brink
of unfolding.

I could not hold them
and I could not hold them
long enough.

It was a sin to let them in.
I did not expect them to stay.
I did not expect their forgiveness
when I turned away.

JOHNNY DAMM

Diagram of a Memory

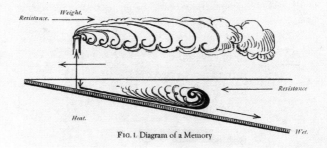

FIG. 1. Diagram of a Memory

Diagram of How I Felt When You Told Me I Look Like Him

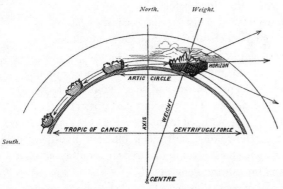

FIG. 64. Diagram of How I Felt When You Told Me I Look Like Him

SAMUEL AMADON

The Brooklyn–Battery Bridge in the Brooklyn–Battery Tunnel

You might make a choice between what descends
with these tiles lined before you, or arcing
forward through a history that is constant against us.
A bridge to block out the dawn. Or monoxide
that passes like breath. My breath. I know all about what's
underground, and I keep my searches for the invisible
there. In the park above, you've got your bike locked
and the chain cut. The stubborn part doesn't say
anything, doesn't need to to
start marching home, ugly block, block of shouting, block
syrupy with flies. I would like to hear about it, but I am
backed into an argument myself
on a coil of cool fall breeze, backed through
seasons into the past, home or near it, in the moment
when I'm as right as I'll ever be bled into
I'll be this right forever. There's no out available
for this character, just a decade producing the present,
warm, and then warmer around him.
It was as if I hadn't seen the harbor, didn't want to
admit it by doing so now. Something
like a pile of books falls over inside me or
the room I'm in breaks off from the house, slides
almost out of view. All things didn't happen
or did. You might've routed a highway so it
crashes through the seventh floor of
a skyscraper, and the moment for that passes by
us still. You can live like a column of light
pours over you, but that's not all you'll see.

RUTH LILLY AND DOROTHY SARGENT ROSENBERG POETRY FELLOWS

Through the generosity of Ruth Lilly and Dorothy Sargent Rosenberg, the Poetry Foundation and Poetry magazine award five annual fellowships to younger writers in support of their study and writing of poetry.

JOS CHARLES

From "feeld"

I

thees wite skirtes / & orang
sweters   / i wont / inn the feedynge marte /
wile mye vegetable partes bloome /
inn the commen waye /   a grackel
inn the guarden rooste /   the tall
wymon wasching handes /
                              or eyeing turnups
/ the sadened powres wee rub /   so economicalie /
inn 1 virsion off thynges /
alarum is mye nayme
                         / unkempt & handeld
i am hors /
i am sadeld /   i am a brokn hors

II

the bit provydes
its hors / the rocke
provyded a boye
blessynge gode / i wantd 1
secrete but fore the rod
inn this / mye longish throte / i kno
no new waye /   2 speech
this / the powre off lyons

III

tonite i wuld luv to rite the mothe inn the guarden / 2
greev it / & as a mater off forme / did u kno
not a monthe goes bye / a tran i kno doesnt dye / just
shye off 27 / its such a plesure to b alive /
inn this trembled soot / u lent / shock is a
struktured responce / a whord lost inn the mouthe
off keepers / & u thum at the mothe / a dozen bes /
i tetherred thees nites / i gathred so manie treees

ALISON C. ROLLINS

Free Radical

Before Gilgamesh invented
the kaleidoscope and Galileo
the Rubik's cube, before the
scimitar-horned oryx went
missing, before the tamarind
trees went bare, before the
stars' eyelids were wrapped
in tinfoil, before the leaves
could gnaw on water, before
electrons made donations,
before the owl wore a mask,
before the wind had a sound,
before the moon had a name
and the smoke a spine, before
the tulips crossed their legs,
before the tongue was
armored, before the ghosts
rode centaurs to riots, before
cyberspace was culled and
belly buttons sown to wombs,
before the taste had an after,
before intellect became
property and thunder
premeditated, before the
New, New World, before a
stone wished to be more
than a stone, before we had a
change of clothes, before the
grass was color-blind, before
the rivers lost their fingers,
and the rain stopped teething,
before the kings were all
beheaded, the gravedigger
neither young nor old, before
a lion was still a lion, before

the girls were all killed, before
the trapeze gave way.   We
hung   suspended in time
by the arches of our curved
feet and this tickled the gods,
tickled them to death.   & I
think our silence cut us loose,
let us go falling from the doubt,
secretly thrilled at the hems
and ever so eager to break.

original [sin]

In ancient Greece, for all her heroes, for Medea ... water meant death.
    —*Jesmyn Ward,* Salvage the Bones

i poured a bowl of cereal,
threw the empty box in the
trash can. granddaddy pulled

the box from the trash,
poured the crumbs into a
bowl, then doused the sand

in milk. he looked down at the
bowl, murmuring about how
he had *survived the depression*. told

a story about asking for hot water
at colored diners, how he would
pour ketchup in cups to make soup.

this was how
i first learned i am
            wasteful.

                    •

i would stand in the bathroom
with my mother. would ask her
why the water in the bowl was

red. she would tell me she
had *eaten beets*. i suppose
i was too young to learn

the truth, milkflowers
spill petals red.

•

in my catholic school of fish,
we took a beautifully wrapped box,
passed it around the class,

unwrapping it piece by piece.
afterwards it was cleverly
explained that the box is

a girl's virginity

the gift we give our husbands.

& who wants a toy that has
already been opened? half
the joy is in untying the string.

this is how i was taught
that at my very core, i am
          ungrateful.

•

i met someone recently,
in an irish bar, who told me
it's about *knowing what i need.*

he said later
*what you need
is a wife.*

that night i prayed to god for *just* a man
and not a man that trails the woe

& maybe this is why god serves me
wakes of *milkman* and *tea cake*

a lip service of sorts
at hand.

●

maybe this is how i end up
throwing good things away:
phd
husband
stepdaughter
stepson
a little tiny baby
        unborn

locked them all in flooding
house with tearful grin.

this is how you
come to know you are
        unclean.

●

at times i smell of rain,
blouse damp with the
cloud's breast milk,

this stomach a
sloshing bowl of
watery swish.

i curse the phantom belly
moon, can still hear the
sound of you in still water.

                    the wind begins to push
a heavy rain, drops spill from
every crevice of the flower.

& then suddenly,
the rain begins to pour.

it always all ways
asks for forgiveness.

a ghost kneels in me,
        asks to be spared.

KAVEH AKBAR

My Kingdom for a Murmur of Fanfare

It's common to live properly, to pretend
          you don't feel heat or grief: wave nightly

at Miss Fugue and Mister Goggles before diving
          into your nightcap, before reading yourself

a bedtime story or watching your beloved sink
          to the bottom of a lake and noting his absence

in your log. The next day you drop his clothes off
          at Goodwill like a sack of mail from a warplane

then hobble back to your hovel like a knight moving
          only in Ls. It is comfortable to be alive this way,

especially now, but it makes you so vulnerable to shock —
          you ignore the mortgage and find a falconer's glove

in your yard, whole hand still inside. Or you arrive home
          after a long day to discover your children have grown

suddenly hideous and unlovable. What I'm trying
          to say is I think it's okay to accelerate around

corners, to grunt back at the mailman and swallow all
          your laundry quarters. So much of everything is dumb

baffle: water puts out fire, my diseases can become
          your diseases, and two hounds will fight over a feather

because feathers are strange. All I want is to finally
          take off my cowboy hat and show you my jeweled

horns. If we slow dance I will ask you not to tug
          on them but secretly I will want that very much.

Vines

there are fat wet vines creeping into my
                    house through the pipes and through

               the walls gentle as blue flames they curl into
my living there is ice in my attic sugar on my
               tile I am present and useless like a nose torn

                    from a face and set in a bowl when
               I saw God I used the wrong pronouns

                    God bricked up my mouthhole
                         his fists were white as gold there were
               roaches in my beard now I live like a widow

every day a heave of knitting patterns
                    and sex toys my family speaks of me

               with such pride *noonesh to roghane* they say
his bread is in oil I thank them for that and
               for their chromosomes most of which

                    have been lovely I am lovely too my body
               is hard and choked with juice like a plastic

                    throat stuffed with real grapes my turn-ons
                         include Ovid and fake leather my turn-
               offs have all been ushered into the base-

ment I'll drink to them and to any victory
                    the vines are all growing toward the foot

               of my bed I am waiting for them to come
under the covers I am the only person still in
               this house there is no one here to look away

Despite My Efforts Even My Prayers Have Turned into Threats

Holy father I can't pretend
I'm not afraid to see you again
but I'll say that when the time
comes I believe my courage
will expand like a sponge
cowboy in water. My earth-
father was far braver than me —
coming to America he knew
no English save Rolling Stones
lyrics and how to say *thanks
God*. Will his goodness roll
over to my tab and if yes, how
soon? I'm sorry for neglecting
your myriad signs, which seem
obvious now as a hawk's head
on an empty plate. I keep waking
up at the bottom of swimming
pools, the water reflecting
whatever I miss most: whiskey-
glass, pill bottles, my mother's
oleander, which was sweet
and evergreen but toxic in all
its parts. I know it was silly
to keep what I kept from you;
you've always been so charmed
by my weaknesses. I just figured
you were becoming fed up with
all your making, like a virtuoso
trying not to smash apart her
flute onstage. Plus, my sins
were practically devotional:
two peaches stolen from
a bodega, which were so sweet
I savored even the bits I flossed
out my teeth. I know it's

no excuse, but even thinking
about them now I'm drooling.
Consider the night I spent reading
another man's lover the *Dream
Songs* in bed — we made it to
"a green living/drops
limply" before we were
tangled into each other, cat
still sleeping at our feet. Allow
me these treasures, Lord.
Time will break what doesn't
bend — even time. Even you.

Angel Nafis

After Monica McClure

Ms. Nafis underwent a repeat pelvic ultrasound today
the final report is not available Preliminary reports
suggest a normal right ovary The left is enlarged
and contains 2 separate complex cysts one measuring
3.6 centimeters the second measuring 1.8 centimeters

B — Black or African-American

•

Angel, most loyal blood. Keep-a-promise,
grow-an-imperfect-garden-blood.
Angel, devoted. Angel, faithful runes of wine
and cardinal. Angel, blank-old-blood, protein
stitched to oxygen. Obstacle course blood,
goddamn know-it-all hand-me-down.

•

Family History:
Mother deceased at the age of 36
Breast cancer diagnosed at the age of 33
Sister has lupus

There are no other known At the time of surgery,
she had a normal-appearing uterus but it was
minimally mobile The posterior cul-de-sac was
obliterated with extensive adhesions

•

Angel, 102-degree fever.
Angel, long-gone lavender in a dirty-water vase.

Angel don't touch me here or there or there.
Can you smell me? Angel unspooled yards

of fabric. Yards and yards of unusable fabric.
Everything has hands, a mouth, everything reaches
across time and tissue.

•

The ovaries were kissing
The ovaries were not identified at the initial point
of the procedure, but after extensive lysis
they were revealed and noted The left fallopian
tube significantly dilated and tortuous

•

Angel, can't you be a good thing?
Angel, on time. Clean scan, Angel.

•

The right ovary also mildly
but not significantly
There was a window in the left posterior
adhesions of the bladder to the uterus
Scattered pigmented lesions on
the pelvic sidewall
above the pelvic brim

•

Angel bowled over like a promise.
Angel howling, adhered to a ribbon of prayer.
Angel, splayed like a galaxy.

Angel, viscera smooth and glistening.
Angel, dilated like a cashed check.

·

After obtaining informed consent the patient was taken
to the operating room She had been placed on foam pads
to prevent slippage while in the Trendelenburg position
Arms tucked at her sides Legs supported in Yellofins stirrups
The cervix grasped with a single-tooth

·

Angel, colon distended, pelvis soaked in saline.
Angel obliterated melon.
Fastened to a dark star.
Lacerated like a web.
Tender witch, misunderstood
by the tide's swift grip.
Ms. Nafis mortal as a rose.
Nobody's mama.

Ghazal for Becoming Your Own Country

After Rachel Eliza Griffiths's "Self Stones Country" photographs

Know what the almost-gone dandelion knows. Piece by piece
The body prayers home. Its whole head a veil, a wind-blown bride.

When all the mothers gone, frame the portraits. Wood spoon over
Boiling pot, test the milk on your own wrist. You soil, sand, and
    mud grown bride.

If you miss your stop. Or lose love. If even the medicine hurts too.
Even when your side-eye, your face stank, still, your heart moans
    bride.

Fuck the fog back off the mirror. Trust the road in your name. Ride
Your moon hide through the pitch black. Gotsta be your own bride.

Burn the honey. Write the letters. What address could hold you?
Nectar arms, nectar hands. Old tire sound against the gravel.
    Baritone bride.

Goodest grief is an orchard you know. But you have not been killed
Once. Angel, put that on everything. Self. Country. Stone. Bride.

JAVIER ZAMORA

Second Attempt Crossing

For Chino

In the middle of that desert that didn't look like sand
    and sand only,
in the middle of those acacias, whiptails, and coyotes, someone
    yelled
        "¡La Migra!" and everyone ran.
In that dried creek where 40 of us slept, we turned to each other
    and you flew from my side in the dirt.

Black-throated sparrows and dawn
    hitting the tops of mesquites,
beautifully. Against the herd of legs,

    you sprinted back toward me,
I jumped on your shoulders,
    and we ran from the white trucks. It was then the gun
ready to press its index.

    I said, "freeze, Chino, ¡pará por favor!"

So I wouldn't touch their legs that kicked you,
    you pushed me under your chest,
and I've never thanked you.

Beautiful *Chino* —

the only name I know to call you by —
    farewell your tattooed chest:
the M, the S, the 13. Farewell
    the phone number you gave me
when you went east to Virginia,
    and I went west to San Francisco.

You called twice a month,
     then your cousin said the gang you ran from
in San Salvador
     found you in Alexandria. Farewell
your brown arms that shielded me then,
     that shield me now, from La Migra.

El Salvador

Salvador, if I return on a summer day, so humid my thumb
    will clean your beard of salt, and if I touch your volcanic face,

kiss your pumice breath, please don't let cops say: *he's gangster.*
    Don't let gangsters say: *he's wrong barrio.* Your barrios

stain you with pollen, red liquid pollen. Every day cops
    and gangsters pick at you with their metallic beaks,

and presidents, guilty. Dad swears he'll never return,
    Mom wants to see her mom, and in the news:

every day black bags, more and more of us leave. Parents say:
    don't go; you have tattoos. It's the law; you don't know

what law means there. ¿But what do they know? We don't
    have greencards. Grandparents say: *nothing happens here.*

Cousin says: *here, it's worse. Don't come, you could be …*
    Stupid Salvador, you see our black bags,

our empty homes, our fear to say: *the war has never stopped,*
    and still you lie and say: *I'm fine, I'm fine,*

but if I don't brush Abuelita's hair, wash her pots and pans,
    I cry. Like tonight, when I wish you made it

easier to love you, Salvador. Make it easier
    to never have to risk our lives.

COMMENT

REBECCA HAZELTON

Civil Affairs

Look, by Solmaz Sharif.
Graywolf Press. $16.00.

In her debut book of poems, *Look,* Solmaz Sharif doesn't so much weaponize language as reveal that language has been a weapon all along. The book's spare and succinct poems are riddled with terminology from the United States Department of Defense's *Dictionary of Military and Associated Terms,* denoted by the use of small caps. This visual cue simultaneously emphasizes and destabilizes a word's generally accepted meaning. As the familiar language we know becomes fraught, our everyday communications are revealed as suspect. By highlighting these specific words, Sharif encourages her readers to greet all words with distrust, mirroring the scrutiny endured by *Look*'s speaker and her family in post-9/11 America.

Penned in the wake of the Patriot Act and years of ceaseless war, these poems evoke the exhaustion of being constantly perceived as a potential threat. In *Look,* this suspicion manifests in obvious and state-sanctioned ways, such as being repeatedly flagged by airport security for pat-downs. It also persists in more subtle forms of erasure and aggression: having one's name constantly mispronounced or being told to be so grateful to be in "this country" as to ignore torture. The psychic toll is evident in "Deception Story," where Sharif writes:

Friends describe my DISPOSITION

as stoic. *Like a dead fish,* an ex said. DISTANCE

is a funny drug and used to make me a DISTRESSED PERSON,

one who cried in bedrooms and airports. Once I bawled so hard at the border, even the man with the stamps and holster said *Don't cry. You'll be home soon.* My DISTRIBUTION

over the globe debated and set to quota. A nation can only handle so many of me.

In these lines, Sharif initially offers up a flattering response to the speaker's affect (stoic), only to immediately undercut it with an ex-lover's harsh and sexually unflattering appraisal (dead fish). Neither interpretation speaks to the underlying cause of this trait: distance. Constant suspicion distances the speaker not only from those around her, but from herself. It's only in the privacy of bedrooms or in the liminal spaces of airports and borders that the speaker's "deception story" is abandoned. That "DISTRESSED PERSON" is one of the DOD definitions is darkly humorous, suggesting that the military complex doesn't share the general public's understanding of common human emotions. Perhaps that's unsurprising; Sharif's use of words such as "distribution" and "quota" shows how language reduces people suffering under politicized scrutiny to interchangeable numbers.

As you might suspect from the book's title, both the act and the term "looking" are under considerable pressure. In DOD terminology, "look" means, "in mine warfare, a period during which a mine circuit is receptive of an influence." Looking can have disastrous consequences, as demonstrated in the titular poem:

> Whereas it could take as long as 16 seconds between the trigger pulled in Las Vegas and the Hellfire missile landing in Mazar-e-Sharif, after which they will ask *Did we hit a child? No. A dog.* they will answer themselves;

> Whereas the federal judge at the sentencing hearing said *I want to make sure I pronounce the defendant's name correctly*;

> ....

> Whereas the lover made my heat rise, rise so that if heat sensors were trained on me, they could read my THERMAL SHADOW through the roof and through the wardrobe.

Sharif's repetition of the lawyerly "whereas" demonstrates how the borders between public and private spaces have been blurred by legislation like the Patriot Act. Legal language tries to be precise, as do drone operators, but either can miss the mark by mistaking one thing for another. When they do, lives are twice snuffed out: first by incarceration or bombing, and then by the act's rationalization (*"No. A dog."*).

In *Look*, martial language infects everyday life, as in "Force Visibility":

> Driving to the cinema
>
> you were yelling
> *This is not*
> *yelling* you corrected
>
> in the car, a tiny
> amphitheater. *I will*
> *resolve this* I thought
>
> and through that
> RESOLUTION, I will be
> a stronger compatriot.

In this poem, Sharif's use of the military term "resolution" casts the argument as war, and her use of "compatriot" casts the relationship as a cause more than a romance. Likening a failing romance to war would be hyperbolic if so much of the book weren't already shadowed by actual war. Here, it seems like the logical conclusion. The arguing couple on their way to view a spectacle are themselves a spectacle, their shouting amplified by the "tiny amphitheater" of the car. This feeling of being on display and exposed to potential danger is rendered even more ominous at the poem's close, when:

> beside us, briefly
>
> a sheriff's retrofitted bus.
> Full or empty
> was impossible to see.

Real power comes from observing without being observed, like the unseen driver, hidden behind tinted windows. It's "impossible to see" whether or not they are a threat to the speaker and her companion, and that uncertainty is its own form of oppression. The only certainty is that there is always more room on the bus.

In the book's standout long poem, "Personal Effects," Sharif's speaker attempts to understand the life and death of her uncle, her Amoo, a casualty of the Iran-Iraq war, by examining what few of his belongings and records she can find. Photographs are scrutinized and unpacked, their analysis supplemented by Wikipedia pages, a quote from Tolstoy, and letters. None of these scraps are sufficient on their own — the Wikipedia pages have dead links, the Tolstoy quote trails away into ellipses, the letters are fragmentary — but this imperfect documentation is the only way to glimpse the uncle and the life he might have had if not for war. This poem, alternatively personal and detached, is especially poignant in its speculative descriptions, as when the speaker looks at photographs of the uncle standing by a tank or holding a bazooka, and imagines his frame of mind ("You're posing. You're scared."), or speculates as to the willingness of his participation in the war:

> You begin to appreciate
> the heft of your boot soles,
> how they propel you,
>
> how they can kick in
> a face —

The shift from a boot's utility to its potential for violence is jarring, intentionally so, as is the admission that the uncle is capable of it. Even more disruptive are the moments in which the uncle's body becomes a kind of surreal interruption:

> *I killed him* she'll say
> in the midst of CIVIL AFFAIRS
>
> he surprises, he arrives,
> eyes taped shut, torso held together
> by black thread, fridge-cold —

The mother's digressive speech is conflated with the sudden appearance of her son's body. It's hard to imagine a more moving demonstration of the incessant intrusiveness of grief.

Sharif's speaker is "attempting my own//myth-making" by reclaiming her uncle's story from any number of pat narratives generated for political purposes. Amoo appears in many forms: as "the amount saved in rations," as "a white archival box//with his PERSONAL EFFECTS" in "a museum/for the martyrs," or as "a 'CASUALTY.'" Finding the real Amoo is an impossible task; none of these narratives suffice. It's telling that the only way for the speaker and Amoo to truly meet again is through an imagined reunion, staged in an airport where confirming identity is a matter of belief and of love, not paperwork:

> I approach you
>
> in the new Imam Khomeini Airport,
>
> fluorescent-lit linoleum, you walk up
> to meet me, both palms
> behind your back
> like a haji. You stoop, extend a hand
>
> *Hello. Do you know who I am?*
>
> *Yes*, I tell you, I half-lie,
> *Yes*. An address, beloved
> lit
> a rooftop of doves
>
>   crouched to launch
> *Yes, Amoo.*
>
> How could I not?

Works and Days, by Bernadette Mayer.
New Directions. $15.95.

In Bernadette Mayer's *Works and Days* history and personal experience overlap and meld in occasionally confusing, often intriguing ways. But if it's a muddle, it's an intentional one. Mayer states in her author's note that "the text is interspersed with seemingly random agglomerations of letters from a daily word game, the jumble." These letters, hovering below many poems, generally read as nonsense, but occasionally surprise us with an intelligible English word (from "May 11": "omcdined endom wreck o demon"). These jumbled letters with their unexpected pops of meaning mirror the experience of reading the book. In saying this, I don't wish to suggest that Mayer's poems are nonsense (they are not), but that the notion of a stand-alone poem doesn't apply here. Many individual poems are opaque until illuminated by the poems around them, and the book very much expects the reader to do the work of arranging those interactions.

For example, reading "Prehistorically in Prehistoric Times" in concert with the next poem, "Waiting for Dave, Megan and Issa," creates a dialogue that is more substantial than the first poem on its own. "Prehistorically in Prehistoric Times" is concerned with what's lost when oral history is traded for scientific knowledge and techno-logical innovation (and, implicitly, written language):

> You couldn't plan to get pregnant
> Nobody yet knew about sperm
> Men thought they were apart
> And nobody knew you could plant plants
> Plants grew wherever they grew
> Where did I see that jack-in-the-pulpit?
> People had memory of all the things
> Their tribe had ever done
> Including in the past they hadn't seen

The poem's presentation of prehistoric memory as encyclopedic and communal, able to reach into a past in which the individual wasn't present, is contrasted with the present-day speaker's inability to remember the location of a just-seen plant. It's funny, though the im-plication that we as a species have lost something precious in favor of scientific knowledge feels like a romanticization of the primitive, es-pecially when that knowledge concerns sexual reproduction. When read alongside the next poem, "Waiting for Dave, Megan and Issa," however, the poem provides an answer to an unasked question:

> Nobody
> Has figured out what to do with nuclear waste
> In Denmark it's to be buried and so nobody
> In future times will unearth it, the whole
> Area will be covered with faux thorns

In this poem, present-day humans are attempting to figure out how to communicate with future humans about dangerous radioactive waste. Scientific advancement is a failure here in more ways than one — there's no solution to the waste but to bury it, and the written word can't be counted on so far into the future. When there's no tribal memory (as in the previous poem), communication is a problem that can only be solved by reverting to pre-linguistic signs: false thorns mean do not enter.

These kinds of conversations across poems occur throughout the book, especially in the book's "days." Like its namesake, Hesiod's *Works and Days*, Mayer's book is a farmer's almanac of sorts. The first page of *Works and Days* tells us this is the "Spring Journal," and many of the book's poems are titled with a month and a day. These entries detail temperature, what's growing or isn't, visits with neighbors, and other small events. Many are small indeed, as in the poem "May 14," where we learn "the birdfeeder fell over again, rain." There's a sameness to these poems that could be dull, yet Mayer mostly maintains the reader's interest through subtle escalations. For instance, the birdfeeder introduces the idea of birds, and two poems later, in "May 16," there's a revelation: the bluebirds aren't bluebirds at all, but swallows. This, she writes, with typical Mayer logic and humor, must be "why they were acting so bluebird-ish." Such variations on the pattern of everyday life are oddly fascinating, especially when inflected by Mayer's often exuberant voice: "it's spring/Or something, a new season called WHOOSH" (from "A New Season").

Works and Days isn't solely concerned with the rhythms of the seasons, but also the rhythms of being a poet. We learn what books the speaker is reading, what classes are taught, and what poets are met. In this excerpt from "May 6," for example, Mayer writes:

Bill Kushner showed up for our reading — me, Phil and Marie reading *Hibernation Collaboration* — and said he'd like to do a collaboration! He was wearing shorts. Also saw John Godfrey, Don Yorty, Keith Gardner, Mitch Highfill and Adam Fitzgerald. We read with inspiring Elizabeth Robinson and ate oysters. A woman named Charity who works for Jonas Meekas kept threatening to jump out the window or just accidentally fall.... Phil nicked his fingers shucking oysters. Saw lilacs! Some leaves are beginning here. Saw ZAM, Zola, Alyssa and Max. It could be Maz. Shazam! Or Mazda.

Some readers will find such moments chummish or even exclusionary, but on the whole, poems like these charm in the New York School tradition. The funny weirdness of the details mitigates any sense of name-dropping for the most part. These, along with many collaborative poems, give readers a glimpse into a vibrant artistic community.

All of this may erroneously suggest that *Works and Days* is mostly quiet and pastoral with a few trips to the big city. Nothing could be further from the case. It is just as often boisterous, personality-driven, and politically radical. One of the book's primary questions regards land ownership. The anarchist catchphrase "property is robbery" recurs in the book, echoing Pierre-Joseph Proudhon, Rousseau, and many others. This concern plays out in many ways. In the "days" poems, the speaker has a growing preoccupation with "GBF," the "guy who bought the field," a new neighbor whose attempts to tame a field into a lawn are met with scorn and distrust. The GBF appears in other poems as well, and when he does, Mayer uses him to critique the concept of property. In "Local Politics," Mayer presents a single-stanza poem which seems to be the product of two overlapping poems. It's nonsense, until the reader learns to read every other line. Just when the reader has the hang of it, Mayer will force the reader to again reassess the pattern. For example:

> The field guy can't stop, he's a lunatic
> (the 1%) rented their land to the 99% of farmers
> zooming around in his bobcat, he
> and extracted crops as rent or even money
> fans the fires of my wrath: property is robbery
> not just a philosophical stance, the Kinderhook
> the farmers dressed as Indians in calico
> Creek Bank is lost to the enemy and poetry ...

The inconsistently alternating, unpunctuated lines unsettle the reader, suggesting that the past and the present are neither stable nor defined. The GBF's manic insistence on ordering the wild field into a tamed lawn seems less funny and more sinister when intercut with a historical example of how property (and its rental) benefits only a small percentage of the population. The poems utilizing this imbricated form are some of the most interesting and challenging poems in the book, presenting at first a jumble, and then, sudden clarity.

Bastards of the Reagan Era, by Reginald Dwayne Betts.
Four Way Books. $15.95.

The subjects and themes in Reginald Dwayne Betts's *Bastards of the Reagan Era* emerge from and are grounded in the formative event of the author's young life: at the age of sixteen, Betts and a friend carjacked a man for a joyride, holding him at gunpoint. When caught, Betts was charged as an adult and served eight years in prison. During that time, he discovered poetry and became a writer. *Bastards of the Reagan Era*, his second book, bears witness not only to one man's experiences in prison, but to the experiences of the community from which he came.

One of the real pleasures of the book is the facility with which Betts shifts effortlessly between elevated diction ("plangency," "coffled"), prison slang and terminology ("Sally port"), and song lyrics. Just as the book's title evokes the eighties, Betts's allusions juxtapose "high" and "low" culture in eighties-era postmodernist fashion. In "Bastards of the Reagan Era," a long, blank verse poem about a prison transfer in which each section shares a title with a Public Enemy song, Betts writes of "the wine-dark asphalt" and directly addresses the reader with: "let/Me tell you how this business began." The latter is a clear echo of "Sing in me, Muse, and through me tell the story," the former a tart refiguring of the most well-known phrase of the Iliad and the Odyssey. With these allusions and the use of blank verse, Betts makes a case that his speaker's trials are as arduous as those of epic heroes, and as worthy of recognition and remembrance. This journey, however, doesn't end with a homecoming:

> But we all dead all dead all dead all dead
> Already, lost and this a voyage from
> Death to death, from godforsaken cell
> To godforsaken cell and I can't stop
> Thinking about before I owned these cuffs.

The unpunctuated repetition of "all dead" reinforces the numbing repetition of incarcerated life. Likewise, Betts repeats "from/Death to death, from godforsaken cell/To godforsaken cell" to suggest that the state of imprisonment (death) doesn't change, regardless of location; one coffin-like cell is the same as another. The line break on "stop" implies that there are more such transfers to come, all equally meaningless. Compared to the often playful accounts of Odysseus's travels, this epic is purposefully bleak and unvarying: "it's all/The same, same fucking thing, a narrative/That ends with cuffs around all wrists, again."

This isn't the only time Betts utilizes repetition. Eleven of the twenty-three poems share the title "For the City That Nearly Broke Me," and four poems have titles beginning with "Elegy." Certain words, like "cuffs" and "black" and "death," repeat throughout the book, drawing connections between race, incarceration, and death. The benefits and the dangers of repetition are evident in the book's three canzones, "Elegy With a City in It," "Elegy Where a City Burns," and "What We Know of Horses." In the first two, Betts takes an already repetitious form and adds even more repetition to it. From "Elegy With a City in It":

> Many gone to grave: men awed
> by blood, lost in the black
> of all that is awful:
> think crack and aluminum. Odd
> what time steals,
> or steals time: black robes, awful
> nights when men offed in streets awed
> us. Dead bodies sold news. What's real?
> Murder cap & all that. The *Post* a jackleg reel
> of it all: black death, awe.
> Chocolate city awash in red:
> 500 bodies lost to morgues.

Spoken aloud, the poem is incantatory. On the page, it's exhilarating to see how Betts finds new variations for the repeated words (awed/odd, for example), or encourages the reader to consider the roots of everyday words (awful = awe full). At the same time, the constant repetition sustained at length is potentially monotonous when the repeated words are used the same way in similar contexts. This dulling effect is compounded when these words appear at the ends of lines, inviting scrutiny that is not rewarded ("men awed/by blood" and "when men offed in streets awed/us").

Throughout the book, Betts emphasizes the disconnect between media portrayals of rhetorical bogeymen and the specific identities of the people he's known. He has stated in interviews that many characters in *Bastards of the Reagan Era* carry their real names or nick-names, allowing Betts to investigate the relationship between a coun-try's rhetoric and the fates of its individual citizens:

> We were in a cloud of rhetoric
> And ganja smoke. The eighties a black cauldron
> That christened Gator, Pookie, and how many
> Others crackhead, fiend, crack baby, more?
> — From *Bastards of the Reagan Era*

Here, young black men lose the names given to them by friends and family and are rechristened as abstract social evils. They lose their indi-viduality and are villainized in service to an overarching political nar-rative. Meanwhile, the stories of people whose successful lives don't fit that narrative go unreported and unremarked upon: "My uncle caught touchdowns for Bladensburg,/where his story. My aunts ain't get high, my mom,/where their story?" ("The Invention of Crack").

Again and again, reading this book, I kept returning to the pro-logue poem, "Elephants in the Fall." This two-part poem describes the naming of Betts's sons. It is lyrical and lovely, detailing the thought that went into each name, the lineages each sprang from, and the aspirations invested in each choice:

> We named
> you after Monk, too,
> because sometimes you have to
> stack legends in a single body
> already big enough for the sound of them
> & we imagined that you gave us
> a different tune,
> a way to bang keys into each
> other until our lives
> filled with unexpected music.

Naming a child is an act of optimism, highlighting the parents' dreams for their child's potential. As a preface to a book in which we see so many young men disappear or die, this hopeful poem serves as a fierce rebuke to complacency in the face of a "world which threat-ens" these young boys with similar fates. How could you, reader, let this happen?

BEVERLEY BIE BRAHIC

Charms, Prayers, and Curses

How Poems Think, by Reginald Gibbons.
University of Chicago Press. $25.00.

Do poems think?

Big question, one that has nagged people at least since Plato was grumbling about the dangerously loose thinking of poets in contrast to the rigor of philosophers. "There's an old quarrel between philosophy and poetry," he said in the *Republic* — but what exactly that quarrel was is moot — not least because Plato's use of dramatic dialogue to make his case was itself poetical.

Much rides, no doubt, on one's definition of thinking. Reginald Gibbons's *How Poems Think* casts the net wide, assuming that poems think in all kinds of ways (abstractly, concretely, etymologically, metaphorically, sonically ...), even poems with the limited attention span of — let me quote, for the fun of it, the beginning of Karen Solie's neck-snapping "The Road In Is Not the Same Road Out":

> The perspective is unfamiliar.
> We hadn't looked back, driving in,
> and lingered too long
> at the viewpoint. It was a prime-of-life
> experience. Many things we know
> by their effects: void in the rock
> that the river may advance, void
> in the river that the fish may advance,
> helicopter in the canyon
> like a fly in a jar, a mote in the eye,
> a wandering cause. It grew dark ...

"Sentences in unpredictable but deep sequence in unpredictable but braced lines," Michael Hofmann says of Solie, who keeps a dozen balls in the air at once and lands them with no-stress aplomb. Here is Gibbons on another poet's comparable flash and dazzle: "[His] poetic thinking moves very fast from one image or allusion to the next ... in what may seem non sequiturs rather than a 'logic' of syntax, line, narrative, setting, or argument." Ashbery? No. Gérard de Nerval.

How Poems Think, however, rests its argument in a quieter place, walking us through a (by now) altogether more user-friendly snippet of William Carlos Williams's 1923 sequence *Spring and All*:

> Pink confused with white
> flowers and flowers reversed
> take and spill the shaded flame
> darting it back
> into the lamp's horn...

Gibbons points to the poem's grace, its doublings, its darting movements, its phoneme repetitions and historical precedents, and to how its words, magically, poetically, seductively, coalesce to produce thought and feeling:

> In his poem, Williams is giving the mere transience of the light from a lamp on a short-lived flowering potted plant its immortal *moment*, and its... immortal... *articulation* in a poem.... In rescuing the humble potted plant from oblivion, Williams performs an ancient poetic role, rescuing for a moment those of us who look at the potted plant with him.

•

Williams's poem is the exclamation point of a book that digs into poetry's rich, layered meaning-making humus. The oldest poems, it recalls, were oral: religious or magical contraptions — charms, prayers, curses — before they became tales of the tribe to be recited and embellished and handed down, eventually in writing, as exemplars (pop wisdom that irked Plato). Gibbons is "fascinated by the antiquity of poetry, or rather, of poetic thinking.... I mean the present-day practice of devices and structures of poetic thinking that were used long ago"; and his book is packed with poetry's teeming underground life, here decaying, there sending up tender shoots. A little word like *cumin* gathers a jarful of observations: "The most ancient version of the word *cumin* was not very different in form and sound from our word.... The spell I might have chanted while holding my little cum-in-seed sack would have been a kind of verbal apotropaic amulet... pushing *away*... a disturbing or dispiriting thought."

Not much breath is wasted exhuming poetry's fall-back mode, the rhetoric of persuasion (consider that diminutive debate, the sonnet, taking its Petrarchan turn or thumping its Shakespearean couplet on the table; or Andrew Marvell's deviously cogent "To His Coy Mistress," or, for that matter, any number of homely but witty poems by our contemporary, Carl Dennis). Gibbons is happiest sifting through the Mallarméan echo chamber of British modernist Mina Loy,

> Onyx-eyed Odalisques
> and ornithologists
> observe
> the flight
> of Eros obsolete
>   —From *Lunar Baedeker*

or Basil Bunting's to-and-fro-ing between Anglo-Saxon and Latin root words. Poems, Gibbons wants us to know, have more ways of thinking than culture-bound readers might dream of, and he lays out his goods for us to contemplate: antiquity's feminine weaving songs, Russian rhymes (that lead, rather than follow or merely ornament thought), nineteenth-century French and twentieth-century English-language poems that glide from sound to sound or, like Russian dolls, nest small words inside bigger ones — "ox" inside "onyx," say. There is a secondary text here, too, about working against the grain — one's own or the assumptions of one's culture — to enlarge one's poetic practice and mode of thinking — something Gibbons set out as a young poet to do:

> In California around 1970, when in my early twenties I was living about fifteen miles inland from the shore of that "peaceful ocean" that was both a body of water and an idea, I was often trying to imagine how to write a poem that would be better, more interesting, than what I had written so far.

How Poems Think's first chapter, part memoir — I'd have welcomed more of this narrative/discursive mode — recounts a formative encounter with Donald Davie, a contemporary of Philip Larkin who came to teach in the US. Davie, Gibbons tells us, deplored the American confessional: "In lyric poetry... what you are doing is making the personal impersonal. This is different from making the private public." Later, Davie would confess his own struggles:

> It is true that I am not a poet by nature, only by inclination; for my mind moves most easily and happily among abstractions, it relates ideas far more readily than it relates experiences. I have little appetite, only profound admiration, for sensuous fullness and immediacy; I have not the poet's need of concreteness. I have resisted this admission for so long, chiefly because a natural poet was above all what I wanted to be.

"Just as the twig is bent the tree's inclined"? No, says Davie. A true poem can be written by a mind "not naturally poetic"

> by the inhuman labor of thwarting at every point the natural grain and bent. This working against the grain does not damage the mind, nor is it foolish; on the contrary, only by doing this does each true poem as it is written become an authentic widening of experience — a truth won from life against all odds.

Gibbons also cites the French poet Yves Bonnefoy on the challenges and rewards of translation as a means of enlarging one's understanding of how poems — and languages — work: "Opposing metaphysics [...] govern and, sometimes, tyrannize the French and English languages. [...] English concerns itself naturally with tangible aspects," whereas French poetry is "*a place apart*, where the bewildering diversity of the real can be forgotten, and also the very existence of time, everyday life and death." The English language, Bonnefoy has said, in his Preface to Emily Grosholz's translation of *Beginning and End of the Snow*, is "so much more aptly fashioned than my own for the observation of concrete detail at a specific place and time, otherwise put, for the expression of the events of a particular existence."

Thus a French writer appreciates the earthiness of Shakespeare or Keats. And English poets — Eliot, Ashbery — absorb French wit, abstraction, and stream of consciousness. *How Poems Think* struck me as particularly illuminating on how the associative thinking of nineteenth-century French poets trickled down into English poetry, shifting it "from representing lived experience, reason, and the world and toward creating an imaginative experience unique to the poem, by means of evocation, ellipsis, allusion, mood, impressionistically presented feeling, and so on." Today, Gibbons speculates,

> perhaps mood too has been discarded in favor of a kind of unmistakable poem-ness ... that has no referent or purpose beyond providing the reader with an experience of a particular way of suggesting a meaning that cannot be thought, or of not being meaningful at all in any expected way.

A beautiful line of verse is all the more beautiful as it means absolutely nothing, a literary friend told Marcel in *Swann's Way* — and Marcel blushed to think that he in his innocence expected of poetry "nothing less than the revelation of truth itself." Rimbaud, whose kaleidoscopic, not-meaningful-in-any-expected-way *Illuminations* John Ashbery not so long ago translated, is described by Thom Gunn (in "Shit") as having

> Coursed after meaning, meaning of course to trick it,
> Across the lush green meadows of his youth,
> To the edge of the unintelligible thicket
> Where truth becomes the same place as untruth.

Making it new? Not necessarily, as Pound, translator of the Tang and the troubadours, knew: some of the new is the old stripped, painted new colors. Poking into cobwebby corners, weaving narrative into discourse, using assemblage, *How Poems Think* is a trove. I read it with a pencil — until I saw that underlining everything was the same as underlining nothing.

The Bonniest Companie, by Kathleen Jamie.
Picador. £9.99.

Reading the Scottish poet Kathleen Jamie and Baudelaire in tandem last autumn I happened on an uncharacteristic landscape poem by Baudelaire and its germ, a poem he composed in his youth, and was struck by how well — if unexpectedly — the sentiment in them corresponded to Jamie's achievement in her new book, *The Bonniest Companie*, as well as in her previous collection, *The Overhaul*. The closing stanzas of Baudelaire's "Elevation" (my stab at a translation):

Behind the anguish and the vast chagrin
Whose heaviness fills and weighs our lives down,
Happy he who with a robust stroke can
Rise towards fields luminous and serene;

The person whose thoughts, like skylarks singing,
Climb freely each morning towards the sky
—Who hovers over life, and effortlessly
Knows the language of flowers and mute things.

Jamie, like John Clare, one of her touchstone poets, is someone comfortable with the language of mute things, who turns readily for inspiration to what, oversimplifying ("everything that is is natural" as A.E. Stallings says), we call "nature." People are less Jamie's thing; they tend to potter about in the wings, gestured to now and then as a "we" or a "you." Her poems are more, however, than felicitous snapshots of epiphanic moments involving deer, birds, or trees. Balanced between descriptions of objective reality and the expression of her own inner life, "The Shrew" (the small mammal) opens the new collection and illustrates Jamie's complexity:

Take me to the river, but not right now,
not in this cauld blast, this easterly
striding up from the sea
            like a bitter shepherd—

and as for you, you Arctic-hatched, comfy-looking geese
                        occupying our fields,
you needn't head back north anytime soon—

snow on the mountains, frozen ploughed clods—
weeks of this now, enough's enough

                    —but when my hour comes,
let me go like the shrew
right here on the path: spindrift on her midget fur,
                        caught mid-thought, mid-dash

Precision, understatement, and humor—the sharp-tongued, sardonic kind also native to the Canadian Anne Carson, perhaps to Calvinist societies in general — are key. Constitutionally modest, Jamie is quick to pull the rug out from under herself: "take me to the river, but not right now"; "enough's enough." One hears the parental voice half-humorously taking the child down a notch until taking oneself down a notch becomes second nature. Jamie's language is as plain as her "cairn of old stones" ("Glacial") but it bristles with perceptual and emotional intensity, with the tones and customs of harsh places.

How does Jamie pack so much into her laconic lines? I ask (mindful of Gibbons's *How Poems Think*), and come up with some tentative responses: 1) by no-comment juxtaposing of alternate realities: here, ultimate things (the sacred river, death), there, sensuous pleasure in the moment's "frozen ploughed clods" and spindrift on fur; 2) by linking herself to a humble creature ("let me go like the shrew"); 3) by peppering poems with feminine signs and diction ("comfy-looking"; that shrew, again, co-opted from its traditional role as a scold: "a bad-tempered or aggressively assertive woman," says my unreformed dictionary); 4) by the sounds and rhythms of her words — what Gibbons, probing historical parallels between poems and weaving, calls "sonic texture" (the nubbly "you Arctic-hatched, comfy-looking geese"); and 5) by gesturing towards pain ("when my hour comes") without making a big deal of it. Much is implicit in Jamie's reticent lyrics and, naturally, all the mute things are thingy — they *are* — but also metaphorical and moral. Some of Jamie's critics speak of her wild creatures as mysterious others, akin to Ted Hughes's roe deer, who "happened into my dimension." I prefer to view them as part of a continuum of life forms, all of them — including, perhaps most of all, the human beings — largely inscrutable. Jamie's realms, as she herself hints in "The Shrew," overlap: the wind "striding... / like a bitter shepherd"; the geese "occupy" like demonstrators or invaders; the shrew is "caught mid-thought, mid-dash" — a traditional female stance, but one whose ordinariness is relatively new to the lyric (the poem performs this state of between-ness by ending without punctuation). Bitterness and comfort, "The Shrew" commonsensically implies, are two sides of life. One senses that Jamie, a philosopher by training, would make a good Stoic.

Kathleen Jamie was born in 1962 in the west of Scotland. *The Bonniest Companie* is her seventh collection. Like *The Overhaul*, *The Bonniest Companie*'s poems are palm-sized: pebbles good for pocketing. Forget Les Murray's "quality of sprawl." This is an Arte Povera — like the sixties' minimalists who made art of scrappy objects, Jamie is subversive in her use of domestic, often feminine, materials; in her stripped-to-the-bare-wood diction and organic forms, as well as in her incorporation of Scots vernacular to mark cultural confidence. *The Bonniest Companie* was written, she tells us in the notes, week by week over the year of the Scottish Independence Referendum. "23/9/14" was composed shortly after voting day:

> So here we are,
> > dingit doon and weary,
> happed in tattered hopes
> > (an honest poverty).
> ....
> > On wir feet.
> Today we begin again.

There is also a translation into Scots "eftir Hölderlin" (easy to read along with Michael Hamburger's English translation) and an overtly political/ecological poem punningly called "Wings Over Scotland" ("Glenogil Estate: poisoned buzzard (Carbofuran)./**No prosecution**") that appropriates media materials.

Honored for her depictions of wild places and creatures that, indirectly, have a fair amount to say about people, Jamie can, when she likes, evoke human tensions more forthrightly, as in two poems, "Moon" from *The Overhaul*:

> *Moon,*
> I said, *we're both scarred now.*
>
> *Are they quite beyond you,*
> *the simple words of love? Say them.*
> *You are not my mother;*
> *with my mother, I waited unto death.*

and "Another You" from *The Bonniest Companie*, in which a sixties tune on the radio reminds Jamie of "Dad's chair" and her mother:

> your knitting bag, all
> needles and pins ...
> ....
> > ... I never

        could explain myself, never
        could explain....
        ....
                    ... It's seven years
        since you died, and suddenly I know
        what the singers say is true —
        that seek as I might, I'll never
        find another you. But that's alright.

"Change, change — that's what the terns scream/.../everything else is provisional,/us and all our works" ("Fianuis"). Rugged and sensuous, Jamie's lyrics belong to and enrich a European tradition that runs alongside the postmodernists, borrowing their techniques — voices like Philippe Jaccottet (Swiss-French) and Tomas Tranströmer (Sweden). Jamie has said that poetry for her is "about listening and the art of listening, listening with attention. I don't just mean with the ear; bringing the quality of attention to the world. The writers I like best are those who attend... Seamus Heaney, Elizabeth Bishop, John Clare." A group into which Jamie's quietly intense poems fit well.

Prodigal: New and Selected Poems 1976–2014, by Linda Gregerson. Houghton Mifflin Harcourt. $16.95.

Linda Gregerson writes long, shapely poems that often come in parts, requiring assemblage. She will begin with an X, jump to a Y, swerve to Z, but eventually the whole shebang falls into place — as associatively-thinking poems do not always do — because Gregerson is good at making connections that might be a stretch for less well-exercised minds: her arguments, however deviously constructed, are sturdy — once you put it all together you can sit down in it. If there are — and there are — strong feelings in these poems, they are governed by an equally fierce intellect. Nothing leaves this workshop that has not been subjected to quality control.

A reader unfamiliar with Gregerson's work might want to start with the selections from her more overtly personal collections, *The Woman Who Died in Her Sleep* or *Waterborne*. Gregerson, storyteller that she is, will often ground austere, impersonal poems with allusions to something *prima facie* autobiographical ("When my daughters/were little and played in their bath"). Still, the reader who starts with the new poems, where the question of authorial distance can be problematic, risks skating over layers of thought and experience that the reader familiar with the earlier poems will intuit. "The Wrath of Juno (the house of Cadmus)," one of the ten new poems, sits as boldly on the page as a bibelot by Marianne Moore, the voices in its faceted quatrains rarely easy to identify:

> It's the children nail your heart
> to the planet, so that's
> > how you nail them back.
> > Alcmena in labor

> for seven days. Think of the man
> who thought up the goddess
> > who thought of that.
> > And pregnant

> Semele, stupid with pride, consumed
> by the flames she had the gall
> > to ask for, though
> > I ought to have known

> that wouldn't be the end of it. *Who'll*
> *rid me of the turbulent mess that comes*
> > *attached to a womb?*

Based on episodes from Ovid's *Metamorphoses*, "The Wrath of Juno" has elements of dramatic monologue, soliloquy, and rant. The speaker rages — to herself? to a listener? — about a long, chaotic experience of the world. On another level she is our contemporary: a woman of a certain age who has learned to be skeptical, not to say cynical, about others ("Semele, stupid with pride,") and the state of marriage, family, the polis, the planet. Gregerson's range (rage) is immense; it encompasses history and literature, an ancient or the latest atrocity, wallpaper, and URLs. Mortgage payments chew the fat with "serotonin uptake" and "geometricians." But when the somewhat autobiographical, if still seven-league-booted ironist dives underground the "I," the "you," and "the girl" become slippery, generalized, universal:

The planets make us what we are,
                              which means
          in turn

          the parts I learned in Tunis and at Delphi must
                              be surface
          agitations on a deeper pool.

          Talk to me, won't you,
                              what was it like
                    in your other life?
                    — From *Pythagorean*

One of my favorite earlier poems in *Prodigal*'s selection is "With Emma at the Ladies-Only Swimming Pond on Hampstead Heath" from *The Woman Who Died in Her Sleep*. "With Emma" is a wry exploration of mother-daughter relations that exposes the resistances and vulnerabilities of both with (I would guess, hard-won) equanimity:

          In payment for those mornings at the mirror while,
                    at her
                    expense, I'd started my late learning in Applied

          French Braids, for all
                    the mornings afterward of Hush
                    and Just stand still,
          ....
          I did as I was told for once,
          ....
                    She's eight now. She will rather

          die than do this in a year or two
                    and lobbies,
                    even as we swim, to be allowed to cut

          her hair.

A great deal happens in and between the lines of these plaited tercets. I admire — oh how I admire — the way the poem meanders reflectively and narratively ("shall we climb/on the raft/for a while?")

but ultimately ties all the ends up with a bow. I note the rich metaphoric content—of, say, braids and the word "cut," and the celebration implied by the poem's penultimate adjective, "honey-colored." Gregerson has a vast reservoir of pity. She also has a reservoir of anger one could drown in. "For the Taking" is a poem about the sexual abuse of a child by a family member: "and we/who could have saved her, who knew// ... //we would be somewhere mowing the lawn//or basting the spareribs... //... we//were deaf and blind." "Failures of attention," as "Good News," another poem in the collection, concludes, loom large in Gregerson.

If Gregerson's poems, especially the newer ones, feel highly-processed, the more one reads backwards in time, the rawer they turn out to be, in their guilts, obsessions, hurts, sorrow, anger. Her multistranded patterns are suited to her anxious, thinky meanderings. They test life from different points along the way, like Proust's shifting views of the Martinville spires; they worry at common human experiences in an attempt to get to the bottom of what Gregerson would probably acknowledge is bottomless, abyssal. The poems in *Prodigal* should be read slowly; if at first they seem to be (as they are) the product of restless, honest, exceptionally well-furnished and rational mind, they are also, it transpires, stuffed with explosives.

CONTRIBUTORS

KAVEH AKBAR is the editor of *Divedapper*. His debut collection, *Calling a Wolf a Wolf*, will be published by Alice James Books in fall 2017 and a chapbook, *Portrait of the Alcoholic*, will be out with Sibling Rivalry Press in January 2017.

SAMUEL AMADON is the author of *The Hartford Book* (Cleveland State University Poetry Center, 2012) and *Like a Sea* (University of Iowa Press, 2010). He edits *Oversound* with Liz Countryman.

BEVERLEY BIE BRAHIC's collection *White Sheets* (CB editions/ Fitzhenry & Whiteside, 2012) was a finalist for the Forward Prize.

STEPHEN BURT is the author of several books of poetry and literary criticism, among them *The Poem Is You: 60 Contemporary American Poems and How to Read Them* (Harvard University Press, 2016).

JOS CHARLES* is author of *Safe Space* (Ahsahta Press, 2016). They are founding editor of *THEM*, the United States' debut trans literary journal. They reside in Los Angeles.

LIZ COUNTRYMAN* is writer in residence at the University of South Carolina and coeditor of the poetry journal *Oversound*.

JOHNNY DAMM* is the author of two graphic chapbooks, *Your Favorite Song* (Essay Press, 2016) and *The Old Man's Illustrated Library: #36 & #5* (No Press, 2015).

ADAM FITZGERALD's poem is reprinted from *George Washington: Poems* by Adam Fitzgerald. Copyright © 2016 by Adam Fitzgerald. With permission of the publisher, Liveright Publishing Corporation.

ISABEL GALLEYMORE's* debut pamphlet is *Dazzle Ship* (Worple Press, 2014). She is working on her first full-length collection.

BRENDAN GALVIN is the author of eighteen collections of poems. *Egg Island Almanac*, a Crab Orchard series prizewinner, will be published by Southern Illinois University Press in 2017.

BENJAMIN GOLDBERG's* poems have appeared or are forthcoming in *Colorado Review*, *Blackbird*, *TriQuarterly*, and *Best New Poets 2014*.

REBECCA HAZELTON is the author of *Vow* (Cleveland State University Press, 2013) and *Fair Copy* (Ohio State University Press, 2012).

BOB HICOK's most recent book is *Sex & Love &* (Copper Canyon Press, 2016). *Elegy Owed* (Copper Canyon Press, 2013) was a finalist for the National Book Critics Circle Award.

ANNA MARIA HONG's fiction and poetry recently appeared in *The Iowa Review*, *The Nation*, and *Fence*. She is a contributing editor at *The Offing*.

LAWRENCE JOSEPH's sixth book of poems, *So Where Are We?* (Farrar, Straus and Giroux), will be published in 2017. He is Tinnelly Professor of Law at St. John's University School of Law.

DONNA MASINI's* poetry collections include *Turning to Fiction* (W.W. Norton, 2004) and *That Kind of Danger* (Beacon Press, 1994).

SHANE MCCRAE is the author of four books, most recently *The Animal Too Big to Kill* (Persea Books, 2015). He teaches at Oberlin College and Spalding University.

LESLIE MCGRATH's* latest book is *Out from the Pleiades: A Picaresque Novella in Verse* (Jaded Ibis Press, 2014). She teaches at Central Connecticut State University.

MICHELLE MITCHELL-FOUST* is the author of *Imago Mundi* (2005) and *Circassian Girl* (2001), both from Elixir Press.

STANLEY MOSS will publish his *Almost Complete Poems* with 7 Stories Press this month.

JESSIE MOTT's art practice includes painting, drawing, sculpture, and writing. Mott received an MFA in Art Theory & Practice from Northwestern University and a BFA from New York University.

ANGEL NAFIS is the author of *BlackGirl Mansion* (Red Beard Press/ New School Poetics, 2012).

VI KHI NAO* won the 2014 Nightboat Poetry Prize for her poetry collection *The Old Philosopher*. Coffee House Press just published her novel *Fish in Exile*.

CONOR O'CALLAGHAN is an Irish poet who lives mostly in the north of England. His most recent collection is *The Sun King* (Gallery Books, 2013). He won *Poetry*'s Bess Hokin Prize in 2007.

EMILY PÉREZ* is the author of *House of Sugar, House of Stone* (Center for Literary Publishing, 2016) and the chapbook *Backyard Migration Route* (Finishing Line Press, 2011).

DONALD REVELL is the author of fourteen books of poetry, most recently *Drought-Adapted Vine* (Alice James Books, 2015), as well as six volumes of translations from the French and three essay collections.

ROBIN RICHARDSON* is the author of two collections of poetry with a third forthcoming with Véhicule Press. She is editor-in-chief at *Minola Review* and holds an MFA from Sarah Lawrence College.

ALISON C. ROLLINS was born and raised in St. Louis. She is a Cave Canem fellow and the librarian for Nerinx Hall. Her poems have appeared or are forthcoming in *Tupelo Quarterly*, *Vinyl*, and elsewhere.

NATALIE SHAPERO teaches at Tufts University and serves as an editor with the *Kenyon Review*. Her second collection of poetry is forthcoming from Copper Canyon Press.

CLAUDINE TOUTOUNGI's* poems appear in *New Poetries VI* (Carcanet, 2015). Her debut collection is forthcoming from Carcanet in 2017. Her plays *Slipping* and *Deliverers* have aired on BBC Radio 4.

JACK UNDERWOOD's* debut collection, *Happiness*, was published by Faber & Faber in 2015. He lives in South East London.

AHREN WARNER* is the author of *Pretty* (2013) and *Confer* (2011), both from Bloodaxe Books, and is the poetry editor of *Poetry London*.

JAVIER ZAMORA is a 2016–2018 Wallace Stegner Fellow. His first book, *Unaccompanied*, is forthcoming from Copper Canyon Press.

* First appearance in *Poetry*.

NEW FROM PRINCETON

Cloth $45.00

Reading Cy Twombly
Poetry in Paint
Mary Jacobus

"This is a beautiful and challenging book. Mary Jacobus takes us into the heart of Cy Twombly's practice, his reading, editing, remembering, and remaking of poetry from Homer and Virgil to Rilke and Paz. In doing so, she illuminates Twombly in new and remarkable ways. I loved it."
—Edmund de Waal, artist and author of *The Hare with Amber Eyes*

Paper $19.95
Cloth $65.00

Corrupted into Song
The Complete Poems of Alvin Feinman
Alvin Feinman
Edited by Deborah Dorfman
With a foreword by Harold Bloom and an introduction by James Geary

"Poetry is making, poesis. And for a time, Alvin Feinman was a maker, a majestic poet who came to embrace his own intolerable limitations, his own dead-end. After long silence, one rejoices in these almost forgotten, rigorous, earthly, purgative poems."
—Henri Cole

Readings, talks on craft, individual
conferences, interviews, gala and more...

Palm Beach Poetry Festival

Poetry Speaks

And special guest:
Charles Simic

Delray Beach, Florida

January 16 - 21, 2017

*Poetry workshops with
America's Award Winning Poets:*

**David Baker • Tina Chang • Lynn Emanuel
Daisy Fried • Terrance Hayes •
Dorianne Laux • Thomas Lux • Carl Phillips
Martha Rhodes**

Apply Now:
w w w . p a l m b e a c h p o e t r y f e s t i v a l . o r g

"The **NATIONAL POETRY SERIES** has been the single most important means for discovering who the best young American poets are."—**MARK STRAND**

"Each poem is a marvel. . . . Range moves nimbly, with acrobatic delight through sonnets, villanelles, anagrams, centro, and the like."
—**TRACY K. SMITH**

"*The Wug Test* is that rare thing—the stunning and necessary emergence of a phenomenal new voice." —**ELIZA GRISWOLD**

"*Not on the Last Day, but on the Very Last* is a stunning achievement."
—**JOHN ASHBERY**

"These poems are no study *in* grief. . . . They leap into our lives, engaging, crackling with wit and intelligence."
—**GREGORY PARDLO**

"At once expansive, agile, and deadly serious, Schoonebeek writes with fugue-like sonic complexity and truly frightening political vision." —**KEVIN PRUFER**

2015 NATIONAL POETRY SERIES BOOKS

Scriptorium by **MELISSA RANGE**

The Wug Test by **JENNIFER KRONOVET**

Not on the Last Day, but on the Very Last Last by **JUSTIN BOENING**

The Sobbing School by **JOSHUA BENNETT**

Trébuchet by **DANNIEL SCHOONEBEEK**

NATIONALPOETRYSERIES.ORG   BEACON PRESS   ecco   milkweed   g   Penguin

THE POETRY FOUNDATION PRESENTS

November Features

Poetry Podcasts | On the *Poetry* Magazine Podcast, *Poetry* editors **Don Share** and **Lindsay Garbutt** talk to contributors and share their poem selections from this issue with listeners.

Poetry Off the Shelf examines **Seamus Heaney's** debut, *Death of a Naturalist*, in the episode **"A First Book 50 Years Later."**

This month *PoetryNow* features **Alli Warren, David Trinidad, Dara Wier**, and **Patricia Spears Jones**. These four-minute episodes are produced in partnership by the Poetry Foundation and WFMT Radio Network.

Podcasts are available free from the iTunes store and on poetryfoundation.org

Harriet News | November's featured blogger, **Tyehimba Jess,** discusses poetics and craft, influence and trends, and the writing life of a poet at poetryfoundation.org/harriet

Learning Lab | View educational resources including a recent article by **Rebecca Hazelton, "Learning the Poetic Line: How line breaks shape meaning."**

Events | Plan your trip to the Poetry Foundation in Chicago to see some of our November events!

Poetry off the Shelf
Lawrence Joseph
Tuesday, November 1, 7:00 PM

Poetry & Music
Stephen Alltop & Josefien Stoppelenburg
Thursday, November 3, 7:00 PM

Open Door Readings
Columbia College Chicago's CM Burroughs & University of Illinois at Chicago's Philip Jenks
Tuesday, November 15, 7:00 PM

Celebration
POETRY Fall PARTY
Wednesday, November 16, 7:00 PM

Exhibition | **Pegasus & Mermaids**
September 23 – December 16, 2016
Monday – Friday, 11:00 AM – 4:00 PM

POETRY FOUNDATION
61 West Superior Street, Chicago, IL
(312) 787-7070

www.poetryfoundation.org

IN MEMORIAM

Richard P. Kiphart

1941–2016

The Poetry Foundation and *Poetry* magazine note with great sadness the passing of Dick Kiphart, former Foundation chair. Dick joined the board in 2012 and was active as Board Chair until his illness forced him to step down just a few months before his death at the age of seventy-five. We all greatly appreciated his leadership of the Poetry Foundation and his contributions to the many other cultural and educational organizations that flourished under his guidance and wisdom. Poetry was only one of the causes that Dick championed. The health and education of children in Africa, music, opera, and arts education were among his most deeply held commitments in Chicago and the global community. We will miss Dick's kind spirit, intellect, wit, and leadership. We cannot thank him enough.